The Disgusted Driver's Handbook

Instructions for Surviving on Roads Infested with Idiots

by Ben Goode

Illustrated by David Mecham

Published by:
Apricot Press
Box 98
Nephi, Utah
84648

books@apricotpress.com
www.apricotpress.com

ISBN 1-885027-09-5

Cover Design & Layout by David Mecham
Printed in the United States of America

As you travel down the highway of life, I sincerely hope that all the cats you run over belong to people that you don't like.

Ben Goode

Contents

1 Fourword

Thirty-some years ago, as a high school student, along with all of the other kids my age, I took Driver's Ed. Having successfully completed the classroom portion, which mostly consisted of flipping spit wads in the dark while a panorama of blood and carnage panned by on the old 16 millimeter projector, the Drivers Ed instructor gave each of us a turn behind the wheel at 5:00 in the morning.

At precisely 1:00 PM on my 16th birthday, having correctly answered 9 out of the 12 questions on the test (with help on the last one from the clerk) I found myself, sweaty palms and all, in the car preparing for the ultimate test-drive with the ornery, jumpy, policeman-guy. On my third or fourth try, I passed the road test and was issued my very first driver's license, complete with a picture of an alien rock formation that was supposed to be me. I was then deemed road worthy, safe to drive. Yes, when I was a kid, this was how it was done.

All my life I have felt perfectly comfortable putting drivers training out of my mind. I have assumed that I could count on the police departments, driver training people and assistant principals to do their jobs. I just figured that this coming-of-age ritual, this time-tested procedure which produced a generation of drivers capable of sitting for hours in unmoving traffic without going ballistic and shooting someone, would go on forever. Imagine my chagrin to awake one morning and discover that I still didn't have a topic to write about in my newspaper column. And since the best way for a journalist to generate interest is to conjure up a controversy or a crisis, and since most of the meaningful, worthwhile crisis, especially those riddled with steamy passion had already been conjured up, I decided to write about the crisis in driver's training.

In addition to the crisis in health care, social security, and foreign lawyers trying to buy corruption on the Geraldo show, I think we need to get all worked up about the horrible quality of drivers today. In addition to worrying about the destruction of the rain forest and the nuclear arms race in Pakistan, we need to add to our worries the thought of what inept drivers our government is allowing on the roads. Therefore, along with Congress, the media, and public education, I am adding to the national list of failures the system which trains and licenses new drivers.

Without having had to worry for many decades about being scrutinized by the kind of investigative writing that I am doing, driving instructors and law enforcement have become slack and lazy. They have let down their guard. If you can imagine, in many states teachers no longer show endless films of bloody arms lying all over the road and various other body parts decorating twisted metal. New students practice driving in a parking lot in cars with automatic transmissions. They watch Walt Disney Movies.

Having missed out on the experience that we older adults all had growing up, I am concerned that many of these new drivers will never become the kind of safe and efficient drivers who could squeeze 13 of their friends into their Volkswagen Beetle, who can both sleep soundly and annoy the other drivers on the road all at the same time, the kind who can talk their way out of a legitimate speeding ticket. It is obvious to me and should be to anyone else out there who has to drive among thousands of idiots, that we are no longer properly preparing drivers for today's rigorous, chaotic experiences on the edge...of the road.

As I thought about my need to get something written for my press deadline, I concluded that a definitive work on driving was clearly needed to help both young drivers and those who have been on another planet for a few decades, prepare for life as it exists on the road today. This book is THE definitive work on driving in the world as we know it.

Because you probably need this information almost as bad as you need your appendix and because we need you to buy this book if we are going to be able to avoid having a real job, we suggest you read it carefully. Then, with any luck, along with the national media, we will all find ourselves in the vortex of a national poor driving scandal. ◆

My other car is a Toilet Seat.

2

A History of the Roads as We Know Them

In order for our readers to be more confused about driving on the roads today, we felt that a little historical background might legitimize some of this high sounding dribble that we are trying to pawn off as useful information. Since we felt that it would be a lot of work to do actual research, we have made up the following:

A preamble to an explanation of how we got our highway system:

In the 1950's, thanks to the popularity and proliferation of automobiles, forward-looking planners began to conceive of a national freeway-

7

highway system. At the turn of one of the centuries, probably the most recent one, I think it was one of the President Roosevelt's who made this system a reality by convincing Congress of the need to have a way to move trucks and television equipment quickly from coast to coast in 2 days or less, in case the Washington Bullets (formerly the Senators) ever made it to the NBA finals and wound up in a 7 game series with the Lakers. While this sounds ridiculous to modern travelers, in those days, in the minds of most congresspersons, it was not all that far fetched. So many signed on. Now, thanks to the wisdom and foresight of these men, if coast to coast travel had not become impossible because of road construction, we could still see these important sporting events in our own homes if we could ever just get the cable people to come out to solve our reception problems.

Since today we have come to take this transportation system for granted, many of you may not be aware that waiting half a day for the pilot car to return would not have been possible if our highway system hadn't had a long history. We would like to share that history with you now. (We would also like to be able to wiggle our ears and burp $20.00 gold pieces, but since we can't do either of those, we will settle for fabricating a history of our interstate highway system.) Here goes.

A history of our highway system:

Our highway system had its beginnings during colonial times as solitary Indians stealthily stole while stalking settlers and game while meandering mindlessly through meadow and mountain as they made their merry way. As they thus cavorted, it became apparent that pretty soon they would either need to move fast enough to outrun disease germs and bullets, or else they would lose the right-of-way. Students of history and watchers of Disney movies know that this was exactly what happened. Very soon settlers from Europe were sacheting, stalking and meandering these same trails.

Sacheting, stalking and meandering was just fine as long as most of the meanderers were just indentured servants, penal colony residents, vanishing Indians, and religious refugees without a life, but as the colonies matured and got into serious industry, rum-running and drive-in movies, they began to recognize the need for better roads. Forward-looking New Deal thinkers led by soon to be president for life, Franklin Elenore Roosevelt, then began a system of disgusting mud drenched roads with deep wagon ruts. While this was an improvement over stalking and sacheting, the roads still meandered quite a bit whenever wagon drivers weren't stuck in the mud.

It wasn't until the advent of the Revolutionary War that military geniuses realized the need for better roads. This need came to the forefront as either General Teddy, "Rough Rider" Roosevelt, Millard Fillmore, or Jimmy Carter, we don't know which, but we're fairly sure that some currently dead president using poor judgment and without wearing his seat belts or a helmet, tried to crowd as many people as he could into his 16 foot water skiing boat so they could avoid the muddy roads to go back to turn off the lights in the old north church. But when some of the boys started splashing on people they tipped over the boat and many of them nearly drowned because they couldn't get their hands out of their coats to swim ashore.

The local Native Americans certainly weren't going to swim out and save anybody since they were really upset at so many states which insisted on continuing to use degrading and pejorative Indian names such as New York (Native Indian meaning: "Yankees", and Cleveland meaning "The Indians") and so many people drowned. They realized that water travel was often not the answer. And since some of them couldn't even remember the question, they pretty much forgot about the roads until after the Civil War.

Your roads at the time of the Civil War

As many of you know, The Civil War was a major watershed in world history. Not only was it the first war to be featured in a major motion picture, but it was also the first war to have a mini series running at the same time as a week long historical documentary. This was confusing to many people who tried to follow all of these shows at the same time because many kept confusing Abraham Lincoln with Whoopie Goldberg, the artist formerly known as Prince with Boy King George and Scarlet O'Hara with the Underground Railroad which motivated the motion picture industry and the academic community to begin a program of revisionist history leading to the corruption of American youth.

This corruption was nearly completed but before the children were old enough to buy cigarettes, just in the nick of time, the automobile was invented. This was followed in short succession by the proliferation of fast food restaurants and the drive-in picture shows or "talkies" as they were then called and before you know it many kids were shiftless, lazy and wanted to die their hair purple and ride skate boards. Since skateboarding was not yet a crime and since midnight basketball hadn't been invented yet and since it was dang tough to make a speedy getaway from a drive-by-shooting on bad roads, many local officials began to look at the possibility of improving the highway system for the children.

At this critical time in history, along came a president, John Travolta, who was capable of taking nearly all of the country's assets and focusing them on this one important social problem: how to destroy the lives of all the people who accused him of doing something illegal to send an unmistakable message to anyone who might disagree with his politics...and still keep his compassionate, nice guy image.

So in order to take their minds off scandal and illicit, steamy relationships, One of the President Roosevelts got everybody working on this massive national highway project. Before we knew it, along came World War I. Not only was it the first war to be so important that it received a roman numeral almost as big as The Super Bowl, but it caused the sinking of the Titanic, which gave movie goers something to watch that was depressing enough to keep their minds off the fact that because of road construction they couldn't go anywhere without an S.U.V. Thus, the modern highway system was born. And sometime later probably, so were you.

12

And so now we have cars and highways and road rage and construction and idiotic drivers and all kinds of stuff that we will proceed to write about in this book. Thank you. ◆

14

3 Modern Rules of the Road

Since everything has changed so much in the years after we got our driver's license, and since so many judgment-disadvantaged lunatics are just pretty much ignoring all of the rules of the road any way, and since there are so many imbeciles who are now allowed to drive on my roads which I own, I felt that the only responsible place to start this book was with a comprehensive, or incomprehensible list of the modern rules of the road. If you plan to continue to drive on my roads, which I own, you better get to know these rules before somebody gets hurt. I didn't make these rules; I don't like them. (I don't even have a cell-phone so I don't get many breaks.) But in order to perform our civic duty, and for the good of the children, we offer:

Modern defacto rules of the road... Offensive driving training for new, ignorant, or irritating drivers:

Rule #1.
Never drive unarmed.

Rule #2.
The current speed limit is whatever everyone else is driving...plus 10 miles per hour.

Rule #3.
If you own a cell phone you can butt into any line.

Rule #4.
Never allow your car to break down alongside the road.

Rule #5.
If you do happen to break down alongside the road, barricade yourself inside your vehicle, pull your gun out from under the seat, load it and wait to die.

Rule #6.
If you have a cell phone, it's okay to drive in the wrong lane against on-coming traffic.

Rule #7.

Every other driver on the road besides you is a registered jerk and a pea-brained lunatic.

Rule #8.

If you own a cell phone, you can drive 15 MPH under the speed limit.

Rule #9.

Every other driver on the road is probably a racist, bigoted, Neo Nazi, who deserves to die.

Rule #10.

If you own a cell phone, you are exempt from any requirement to ever yield right of way.

Rule #11.

Every other driver on the road is devoid of so much as even one molecule of the lowest kind of human intelligence. They operate on purely instinctive behavior and are incapable of rational thought or normal human feelings.

Rule #12.

If you have a stereo system which is powerful enough to make the windows and doors on your car bulge out on all the bass notes, and which can cause an avalanche whenever you drive by a snowy mountain...or in the absence of snow can cause rocks to crumble, and which can cause downtown store windows to shatter, and which will cause permanent ear damage to people driving in nearby cars with their windows rolled up, you are required to crank the volume all the way up at all times.

Rule #13.
If you own a cell phone, you can change lanes without looking or signaling. Other less important drivers are required to move out of your way.

Rule #14.
If you drive a clunker car, you are required to put a minimum of 5 stale bumper stickers on the back.

Rule #15.
If you own a cell phone, you are allowed to glide through stop signs.

Rule #16.
People with "Mean People Suck" stickers on their car need to be hunted down and given a therapeutic group noogie.

18

Rule #17.

Every other driver on the road is evil. They most likely are returning home from just having sold heroine or cigarettes to a bunch of kids at a day care facility.

Rule #18.

If you own a cell phone, you are allowed to weave back and forth all over the road.

Rule #19.

People who have "Humans aren't the only life on the planet, they just act like it" bumper stickers on their car won't mind if you shoot them or run over them to make more room for the other species.

Rule #20.

All other drivers on the road, except for you, are unqualified and most likely driving under the influence, on a license that has been revoked. They are also stupid, ugly and rude. ◆

 # An In-depth Analysis of Speed Limits

Being the kind of guy who drives 80,000 miles a year, I like to get from point A to point B as quickly as possible. In my travels, I have observed that many speed limits seem to be artificially low. Take for example, most roads in the state of Oregon (State motto: "If you were a whale, or a spotted owl, which you're clearly not, you might get some respect"). You're driving along on this freeway-looking place with 4 wide lanes and few other cars. You naturally assume that the speed limit would be 75, but because you know you are in Oregon, you guess it's probably only 65. Just to be sure, though, you're keeping your eye out for a speed limit sign...when you spot one...and it says 35 M.P.H. Really!

21

You know that even in Oregon, the only way they could justify this low of a speed limit on this road would be if there was some really dangerous and unusual hazard, like that this is a spot where huge Tyrannosaurus's recently regenerated from bugs preserved in prehistoric sap leap out of crevices that you can't see in the road and devour your car...or else you need to be able to stop quickly to avoid collisions with alien space ships which have chosen this highway as their main landing spot...or else they're concerned about earth quakes...or possibly a need for major infusions of extra ticket revenue to fund their experimental social programs like providing marijuana to 4th grade students for medicinal purposes, and so you drive with extreme caution. And you are mighty glad you did too, because while you didn't see any aliens or prehistoric beasts, you saw hundreds of other, less cautious drivers being pulled over by the Oregon Highway Patrol.

As you can see, speed limits, to the uninitiated, can be one of the most confusing aspects of driving, especially now days when the highways and roads in our country are so dominated by the blind, the deaf, illegal aliens, and the functionally brain dead, who are also blind and deaf. So that you don't become confused, we've made the following descriptions of the rules concerning speed limits:

25 MPH

This is a "residential" speed limit which means that "residents" have an average AGE of 25. It has nothing to do with your car's recommended speed. You will observe that some residents' near schools have an average age of only 20 or sometimes 15 while some are as old as 95. You will therefore need to adjust your speed to the conditions. For example, sometimes a safe speed is "0" such as when two old codgers have parked their pick up trucks so they can shoot the breeze and they're blocking both lanes so you can't get past. At other times the speed limit will be 120 such as when you are trying to score 10 points by running down the neighbor's cat, (See chapter 5) or to annoy a neighbor kid.

35 MPH

This sign generally means that you should drive around 50 or so to avoid having other cheery drivers give you the internationally recognized "You're #1" salute.

55 MPH

This speed limit is a mistake. You should know that there is no where on the planet where 55 is a reasonable speed. It is either too fast to be safe, such as in the parking garage, or else it is artificially slow such as on highways. You can safely assume that wherever you see a 55 mph sigh, it's a joke...except in Oregon where there is no legal sense of humor. In 55 mph zones, be sure to drive at least 75 miles per hour or other irritated drivers will assume you are not paying attention because you are talking on your cell phone and they will shoot holes in your license plates.

75 MPH

As all veteran drivers know, 75 miles per hour really means that most policemen won't cite you if you are going 85 or less, unless it's the end of the month and they haven't made their quota, or you are in Oregon, where, because of a genuine feeling of moral superiority, they have an obligation to cite you even if you are going only one mile over the limit for your own good to improve your character and to save the rain forest and the Ozone. Therefore, as long as you don't already have lots of points and if you aren't on the verge of losing your license, wherever roads are posted at 75, feel free to drive as fast as your car will go.

NO SPEED LIMIT

This only happens in Montana and the Auto Bon in Germany and in heaven. If you should find yourself on a highway with no speed limit, savor the moment, freedom loving social engineers will have the problem fixed soon enough...or else you'll discover you've died and been sent to the wrong place and in the blink of an eye, you'll be back in Oregon.

SPECIAL SITUATIONS:

1. When you don't want to draw attention to yourself: If you are driving a car filled with illegal aliens or if you have a load of illicit drugs, since things could go badly for you if you are pulled over, you might want to exercise a little extra caution: The Federated Organization of Pea brains (or F.O.P.) suggests that you do things a bit differently so as to avoid drawing any unwanted attention to yourself. They recommend that you drive a huge car the age of Bob Hope, at slightly below half of the speed limit. They also suggest that you ignore stop signs, and whenever you change lanes, do it without signaling. If you should get pulled over, without rolling down your window, hold your counterfeit green card up to the wind shield and smile.

2. Driving in the presence of policemen: There are times when you're driving along at prudent freeway speeds of 20-30 MPH over the "good humor suggestions" posted alongside the road, dreaming about cheese sticks, when all of a sudden, you find yourself in a clot of slow cars which is behaving very strangely and beginning to annoy you. Each driver is staring blankly out the side window whistling, appearing to be quite content to drive at 10 MPH below the posted artificially low humor speed suggestion non-limit. You know that driving like this is completely unnatural for humans.

Just before you are about to break out your old hand gun and start shooting into the air to get things moving, you suddenly spot the problem: in the front of this unnatural clot, looking very much like a construction pilot car is a black and white police car.

Whenever this happens to you, follow this procedure precisely as outlined: You should quickly slow down to the speed of the rest of the cars while you think of a tune to whistle, all the while staring blandly out the window. Then gradually, but imperceptibly, begin to speed up 1-MPH at a time. If you do this correctly, it will take about 45 minutes to weave your way through the

26

clot without drawing undue attention to yourself. Then, when you are about a mile ahead, a safe distance from the radar gun, return to normal freeway speed. ◆

Lost your Cat? Try looking under my tires.

5

The Point
System

It can be a frustrating thing to be driving in your car and to spot an opportunity to swerve skillfully in order to try and run over a neighbor's cat or to risk life and limb to door that rotten little neighbor kid while he's riding his skateboard, and then after being successful at one of these, having to wonder how many points you should be awarded for the effort. Therefore, we believe that an essential part of the new world order should be a universally accepted world-wide highway point system.

The following is the system compiled by Farley Hoyl, the illegitimate son of the famous Hoyl card family who was commissioned to put together a comprehensive, universally used automobile point system. If you have been using a different point system, you should stop now. And be sure and mark all points that you earn conspicuously on the bumper or fender of your car.

Universal Point System of the World

THE OBJECT RUN OVER	POINTS
AN INSECT	1.0
A TOAD	1.0
A LARGE INSECT	1.5
A REALLY LARGE INSECT	2.0
A TWEETY BIRD	2.5
A MOUSE	3.0
A STANDARD DOG	5.0
THE GHOST OF ELVIS	5.0
A SKUNK	10.0
A STANDARD CAT	10.0
A GOOSE	10.0
A COYOTE	15.0
ASSORTED VERMIN	20.0
A CUTE LITTLE YAPPING, WORTHLESS, PAMPERED, MANICURED DOG	25.0
AN ELVIS IMPERSONATOR	50.0
A BASKETBALL REFEREE	50.0
A PORCUPINE	50.0
ONE OF YOUR IN-LAWS	50.0
A FLUFFY, PAMPERED CAT WHO'S NAME YOU KNOW	65.0
AN ENVIRONMENTALIST	100.0

(If you also clip the tree he's chained to, subtract 5 points)

THE ASSISTANT PRINCIPAL	100.0
A WHALE	100.0
AN ALIEN SPACECRAFT	200.0
A LAWYER	400.0
ANY LAWYER FROM THE O.J. SIMPSON DEFENSE TEAM.	500.0
ELVIS	500.0
A TELE-MARKETER	700.0
A TERRORIST	1000.0
A POLITICIAN	1500.0
ANY POLITICIAN WHO VOTED NOT TO ABOLISH THE I.R.S.	2500.0

Penalty Points**

You can have points taken away for hitting any of the following:

A LARGE ROCK	-5.0
A PHEASANT	-5.0
A POTHOLE	-5.0
A VERY LARGE POTHOLE	-10.0
A DEER	-10.0
ONE OF YOUR RELATIVES	-15.0
AN ELK	-20.0
A MOOSE	-25.0
AN HONEST WORKING PERSON	-100.0
A BUFFALO	-100.0
A BRIDGE ABUTMENT	-1000.0

**If you hit the Grand Canyon, a Major Ocean or other significant type of geography you may be disqualified altogether.

31

My other car is a dirt clod too.

6

Driving with an Attitude

One of the principle causes of mental illness, anger, depression, death and hives in America is driving in traffic...surrounded by idiots. That's why when you are on the road it's so important to keep a level head. In order to help you, my enraged and frustrated readers, keep a healthy attitude, assuming that driving while being heavily medicated is not an option for you, we would like to share these coping skills for dealing with maniacs behind the wheel. This is especially important because recent public opinion polls have shown that many people feel that other drivers on the road need to be shot with automatic assault weapons which are now illegal.

First, though, we need to explain why it is that a person who appears to be perfectly competent to cook toast or pick up a newspaper gets behind the wheel of a 6000 pound automobile and becomes a raving lunatic...To do this, I contacted Dr. Herald Putz, world renowned, preeminent driving psychologist to get an expert scientific perspective.

As luck would have it, while he was driving over to talk to me, some little old lady who had just charmed the people at the drivers bureau into letting her keep her license against their better judgment, made a sudden lane change and forced his car into the median. Since he didn't have his shot gun loaded, he had no alternative but to try to retaliate by ramming her 1968 Pontiac Bonneville, which still had the dice hanging from the mirror, with his 1988 Hyundai Excel. As you have probably imagined, traveling at freeway speeds, the other driver mistakenly thought that the scraping sound caused by this tiny foreign car bashing into her very large car might be trouble in the transmission. So, to check it out, she quickly shifted into reverse.

Dr. Putz and his Hyundai are now an insignificant part of some woman's under carriage and as we speak are cruising around Scottsdale, AZ as part of a 1968 Bonneville. So we have drawn our own conclusions about what causes people to transform when they drive. Here are just a few...

First, it seems logical that since we know that most forms of bad behavior are genetically caused, they are beyond the control and, therefore, the personal liability of the individual, we have determined that nearly all lunatic driving is caused by mutated anger genes.

Second, since most deviant behaviors not caused by genetics are a result of slavery in the 17th century, this makes the federal government responsible to come up with a program to pay for these past mistakes...or to at least make voters feel like they're doing something to assuage their guilt. Like most other social problems, a good place for them to start is probably by taxing and penalizing all white males relative to the rest of the population because their ancestors knew people who owned slaves and shot Indians...and by giving poor, non-white and non-males all the good jobs and some kind of tax credit.

There. Knowing what's at the root of the problem, we can go to work to eradicate bad driving altogether. This can best be done by creating regulations requiring side impact airbags on all vehicles down to skateboards and requiring all congresspersons to wear helmets while skiing.

Unfortunately, since the Federal Government will certainly take at least a couple of decades to study the problem before doing anything to solve it, and since the problem won't wait, as an interim solution, we hereby declare ourselves the bad-driver police and scholarly experts of the universe. We don't carry a gun. We don't pull people over. (We would just get beat up all the time if we did.) Instead, for a few million in government grants, we will voluntarily drive around looking for people who make serious driving errors like driving only 5 MPH over the speed limit in front of us or failing to signal when they cut us off...and we display the internationally recognized signal that they are "#1" with us.

By showing our contempt for all of the other drivers on the road in this manner, we feel that we are doing our part to make other drivers aware of what imbeciles they are, at the same time helping all drivers to promote "offensive driving."

How to respond when you get the finger because you are a rotten driver:

Let's say that you're driving along and, through no fault of your own, you inadvertently change lanes without looking in your rear view mirror, looking over your shoulder, and without signaling. Imagine further that there just happens to be someone else driving along in that lane in the precise spot where you just drove your automobile, who, up until now, was enjoying his or her drive and had every intention of continuing to drive in that lane, but who now has been forced to drive at freeway speeds across people's lawns. Let's also assume that they are unhappy about it and that the bad driving police are nowhere to be found. The question is; "What should you do?"

One of the best options I have found when you do something really bone-headed, the kind of thing that when someone else does it to you, you will go to great lengths to do them harm, is to suddenly slump over the steering wheel and act as though you are having a heart attack which is impairing your ability to drive responsibly. If you can contort your face and look like you're in real pain, this will usually buy you some time and occasionally even get you some sympathy.

However, since you can't keep your eyes closed and stay in that position for long without possibly wrecking your car and killing yourself, you will need to have a back-up plan.

What you could do next is pull the sawed-off shotgun out from under the seat and wave it menacingly at the other driver while making up imitation gang symbols until they speed off down a side exit in an obvious panic, or until they pick up on the big joke and you get a reluctant smile out of them. ◆

7

Bumper Stickers

Few things in life are more annoying than a stale bumper sticker. We understand this. Try these:

> **Just Because I Drive A Small Car Doesn't Mean I Can't Be A Big Jerk**

> **Honk if you want to get beat up**

> **I'd rather be...someone of consequence**

Caution: I have forgotten that I have a rear-view mirror

I'm so cute I never get tickets

My other car is a toilet seat

Honk if you're an illegal alien

Will Whine For Food

I go from Dweebe to Wing-nut in 2.5 seconds

Caution: I change lanes without warning

I'd rather be sleeping... Hey! I am sleeping!

Lost your cat? Try looking under my tires.

Stop Global Whining

Honk if your underwear's in a wedgie

This truck will pull in front of you
on all hills

Tired? Fatigued? Depressed?
Get some sleep.

Honk if you want your car stolen

Perverts do it in the White House

My other car is a couch

**Fathers Against Radical Teenagers
(F.A.R.T.)**

Horn Broken...Watch For Finger

**Caution: my turn signal has
never been used**

**Honk if you're not getting
enough attention**

Jerks are people too

**I May Look Smart, But I Tend To
Drive Stupid**

**If you're in a hurry I drive 10 under
the speed limit**

Honk if you're an Idiot

My honor student can beat up
his little sister

Entomologists make better lovers

My grandma went to Las Vegas and all she
bought me was this Mazerati

Small Animals Beware

Honk if you fall asleep and hit your head
on the steering wheel

I'm armed and I'm ornery

Politicians are people too

Will Sue for food

Coping with Construction

The other day I witnessed a remarkable change in the area where I live. I had been sitting for 2, 3, maybe 10 hours in my pickup with the windows rolled down in the 94 degree heat waiting for the pilot car to return so I could finish what would have been my 10 minute trip to the post office when I was shocked to see all of the construction workers jump up and start moving all at once. While I didn't see any actual work being done because they were just milling around acting kind of weird, I was nonetheless thrilled as it became apparent that many of them were still alive and some may have been capable of eventually doing some constructing.

As I watched, I got more and more excited and optimistic about to what good use they were putting our tax dollars, until I noticed that these construction workers were all beginning to move to another spot and that one by one they were lying down to rest again. It turns out that they had all chosen a hill of biting ants to sit on while they ate their lunches. And now, after having spent all that energy being stirred up, they were again back to normal, fixin' to get ready to start thinking about planning to contemplate doing some work.

We all understand that without construction there would be no roads and that without roads, there could be no potholes. Without potholes, many construction workers would have no jobs and without jobs, there would be no work, without work, there would be no food and without food, of course even all the drivers would die and if everyone died, there would be no need for construction. And so you see, if you look at things scientifically and analytically, construction can be good. And since it will never be completed in our lifetimes, we must find ways to cope. With this in mind we offer the following things you can do while waiting in construction:

Things to do while waiting for the pilot car to return:

1. Catch up on your sleep. In fact, you can probably get enough sleep to get everyone you know caught up by proxy.

2. See if you can invent at least 100 creative ways to tie your shoe laces.

3. Write letters to your congressperson.

4. Using your nose as a brush and the frosting from the brownie in your lunch box as paint, make beautiful "greasy smudge art" on your car windows.

5. Visualize world peace.

6. Locate a pin and use it to make yourself a new dinosaur tattoo. Your belly button can be its mouth.

7. Read the complete works of William Shakespeare.

8. See how high you can stack the broken sun flower seed shells on the floor of your car.

9. Booger sculpture.

10. Write a research paper explaining Einstein's theory of relativity.

11. Get out and introduce yourself to the next 200 or so drivers waiting behind you in line. . . or better yet, invite them to play twister!

12. Go on a nature hike.

13. Work on your yodeling or some other worthwhile skill.

14. Pull your sawed off shotgun out from under the seat and practice shooting the chrome off from the cars in front of you.

15. Work on your "Guiness Book of World Records" collection of belly button lint by asking people in the other cars to donate theirs.

16. Throw rocks at sleeping construction guys and see if you can rouse them.

17. Learn to dance the polka using a driver from one of the cars as a partner.

18. Put your finger over one nostril and using the other one, count how many gnats and mosquitoes you can inhale.

19. Memorize the U.S. Tax code.

20. Catch and train the birds, rats and other vermin you see along the roadside to do tricks.

21. Write your masters thesis or doctoral dissertation.

22. Clean up road kill.

23. Find 3 other drivers who can sing and work on a barber shop quartet.

24. Pick up litter.

25. Polish the underside of your car or truck until you can see your face shining in the differential.

26. Try to imagine all of the business deals going sour while these thousands of people sit helplessly. Then, in your mind, imagine what you could do with all that money that's been lost.

27. Using extra parts that your car doesn't need, design and build a radar jamming system just in case you ever get past the construction. This will help keep you from getting tickets while you're speeding along at twice the speed of light trying to make up for lost time.

There, now quit whining and never say that there's nothing worthwhile to do while you're waiting for the pilot car to return. ◆

I've forgotten I have rear-view mirrors. . .

9

Why Otherwise Pretty Dopey People Become Total Imbeciles When They Get Behind the Wheel

For many years, I have been amazed at how an average person, someone who can barely chomp on his gum when he talks, a person who is always saying something crude or completely inappropriate in the worst possible places, someone who has absolutely no sense whatsoever of good taste, color coordination, which NBA team he should cheer for, or what is going on around him...why you get a person like this behind the wheel of a car controlling two tons of steel which can kill people and he seems to mutate into a complete idiot. Whatever small particle of good judgment previously existed completely rots away. Instantly he or she becomes transformed into a bumbling, raving and often angry lunatic. Why is this so?

As you can probably tell, from reading chapter 6, I have thought about this a lot. And I have come up with some more food for thought, some stuff that we can do some serious speculating about. Consider these:

36 more plausible reasons why normally stupid people instantly become complete idiots when they get behind the wheel

1. His underwear is too tight.

2. She's on her way to a drive-by shooting.

3. He recently found out that his owner is having him neutered.

4. Earlier today while swerving to hit his neighbor's cat, he missed it, lost control of his car and drove through his own flower bed, ruining his begonias.

5. She thinks she's fleeing molten lava or a killer bee plague or something.

6. He just had a trendy new nose-ring drilled through his head and it hurts.

7. He has been constipated for 4 years.

8. She just turned her mom, dad, and grand parents in to the IRS and instead she got audited herself.

9. She just witnessed her dog, Sparky, get run over by a riding lawn mower.

10. He is listening to rap music.

11. Deep down inside, underneath that obnoxious exterior, he really is a big jerk.

12. During her therapy her shrink just recommended suicide as an option.

13. She was just sexually harassed by The President and so now she knows that her reputation is about to be trashed and her career ruined by his operatives.

14. He just discovered that The President accepted bribes from the government of Bora Bora to get chemical weapons. Now he knows that presidential operatives will be busy destroying his reputation and career.

15. He just found proof that The President is a cross-dressing alien who is into kinky alien stuff and so now he is just waiting to have his reputation and career destroyed by operatives.

16. She just discovered a plot by The President to use his computer program to siphon off social security funds and deposit them into his legal defense fund so now she can be sure that his operatives are planning to destroy her reputation and ruin her career.

17. This morning someone dropped a 25-story building on his foot.

18. The corns on her feet just exploded.

19. He has been driving around in his "79 Datsun looking for a Cadillac to run into so he can collect insurance and he just missed the Caddy and ran into a parked police car.

20. She spent the weekend buried in an ant hill and happened to have jelly beans in her pocket.

21. He is wearing underwear made of spun glass attic insulation.

22. She just went in for her annual rabies vaccination booster shot and the nurse wasn't paying attention. She kept injecting until her hemorrhoids became inflated.

23. He just finished plucking his nose hairs.

24. His wife put jalapenos and Drano in his peanut butter and jelly sandwich.

25. She thought she poisoned the neighbor's yapping mutt but instead, she missed the dog and killed all wildlife within a 2 mile radius.

26. His mom makes him listen to oboe music whenever they drive in the car.

27. He was just approved by The Senate to be in The President's cabinet and now he knows it's just a matter of time before he becomes indicted.

28. She is the wife of the president and wrestling with how to justify standing by this creep.

29. He just had the warts burned off his ears, hands, left shoulder and tongue.

30. He just drank a perfectly good $79.00 bottle of Rogaine and didn't know you were supposed to put it on your head.

31. He just woke up from being beaten senseless by his bookie for back gambling debts.

32. Her kids took the last of her stash of

crystal meth, crack, and medicinal marijuana to their friends' party.

33. Someone just abandoned 10 pounds of fleas in his car.

34. Her brains leaked out her ear.

35. He stole the car and just discovered there's a corpse in the trunk.

36. Someone just put lots of sticker weeds in his shorts.

While there may be one or two reasons we've overlooked, this should get most of the legitimate ones. ◆

More inspiring bumper stickers

My other car is a dirt clod

Diplomacy is for people who don't know how to beat everyone else up

This is how I drive; get used to it

Honk if your kid is crying in the back seat so you reach back and accidentally bump the horn

Mean People Are Mean People

Skateboarding...is a waste of time

10 The Car You Drive Makes a Statement About You

You are probably aware that billions of government dollars are spent each year on scientific research, much of it by people who are real good at locating government grant money but who otherwise couldn't find the working end of a shovel, who don't know the difference between a soiled Kleenex and caviar. What many of you may not know is that scientists have spent millions of tax dollars analyzing your brain. One part of this valuable research has dealt with the kind of car you drive and what your car reveals about your personality.

The following is a bit of similar research which we made up, but which many of our readers may find plausible anyway. In spite of its deficiencies (mainly, it's all a bunch of hooey) it does provide quite a bit of trivial and questionable information. Unlike many well known world wide information superhighways, right now we're not selling anything. One other thing that you will notice, should you take the time to read this, is that our study, while not costing any federal money, also includes a psychic forecast of your future at no additional cost. As an added bonus it is not X-rated.

We suggest that you go down this list and find your car and then read the personality profile describing you or your significant other and discover their dark secrets.

If you drive this:

An 18 wheeled semi named Betsy Lou.

It means this:

You don't get enough sleep. You're a little over weight. You know where all the good, cheap eating places in America are. All small animals within half a mile of the road tremble in fear. This year they will pass another set of taxes and regulations even more baffling than the last ones which were

designed to give
highway patrolmen a
few more reasons to use
you as an additional
revenue source, which
will help to dig your
financial hole faster and
deeper than it is now.

If you drive this:
A VW Microbus.

It means this:
You are most likely a
promiscuous, burned-
out, foul-smelling hippie
throw back to the 60's,
who's into Frisbee and
who has head lice and is
paranoid about any one
in law enforcement and
so you refuse to go over
30 miles per hour up
hills.

If you drive this:
A Cattle truck.

It means this:
You're in an ag-related
business, broke, and on
the verge of bankruptcy.
Very soon Oprah and
Geraldo will team up to

produce an expose documenting the fact that many of your chickens have bad personal hygiene which will destroy the poultry and soy bean markets. At the same time, your costs will go up and prices will go down.

If you drive this:
A Vespa Motor Scooter.

It means this:
You have a pocket protector and thick horn-rimmed glasses. You don't go out much and your hobbies include collecting mold spores and fungus.

If you drive this:
A 1983 Ford Station Wagon with 290,000 original miles.

It means this:
Your other car is a cattle truck (see above)... or... you still have 8 kids at home... Very soon Oprah and Geraldo will team up to produce a documentary expose

62

exposing the fact that the man who sprays tofu-based vitamins on your soy beans has poor personal hygiene and hates all whales which will destroy the poultry and soy bean markets. Meanwhile, your costs will go up and prices will go down.

If you drive this:

A pickup truck with a camper and a "Work is for people who don't know how to fish" bumper sticker.

It means this:

You are retired and right now you're not good for much. You hardly ever get to fish because you have to work... or else you're too tired and it's too much effort.. or because your wife has an endless "honey do" list.

If you drive this:

A Mini Van.

It means this:

You spend your Saturdays at little league and soccer games and

63

you're an officer in the P.T.A. While it is difficult for you to comprehend, very soon those kids will cost you many times more money than they do now. Some may even be worth it.

If you drive this:

A late model sports car.

It means this:

If you're over 40: You wear a toupee, have gingivitis and suffer from poor color coordination. You sincerely believe you're it. You're contemplating leaving your family because they're just holding you back. People talk about how goofy you are behind your back. If you're under 35: You have industrial quantities of cat fur in your treads. People want to be seen driving your car.

If you drive this:

A light blue 72 Dodge Dart or it's equivalent.

It means this:

Your dad says you should just be glad you have this to drive. When he was a boy, he had to ride a goat. (At least you know that the girls or boys don't like you just for your car.) You'll be graduating from high school soon and so then you'll be rich enough to buy any kind of car you want.

If you drive this:

A late-model SUV.

It means this:

You are cool. Everyone wishes they were you. However, you are the principle cause of Ozone depletion, global warming, the homeless, and you are fouling Al Gore's environment and he won't stand for it. Very soon he will pass a law requiring that if you choose to breathe that you exhale nitrogen, oxygen and ozone.

If you drive this:

A Mercedes Benz, Acura or other foreign luxury car.

It means this:

You are optimistic that a big deal will close just around the corner bailing you out of this horrific financial bind you're in...or else you're some kind of celebrity probably on drugs. "If you all stick to our story, they can't prove anything."

If you drive this:

A Red Jeep CJ-7 with a black hard top and fake cowhide seat covers.

It means this:

Either you are Dave Mecham, or else you are somebody else who drives the same kind of car he does.

If you drive this:

The Star ship Enterprise.

It means this:

Either you are Klingon or you are a pasty-green skinned android.

If you drive this:

A Toyota compact car.

It means this:

This covers everyone else in the United States. Congratulations. You are a standard, garden variety Homo Sapien. ◆

11

Geezing Behind the Wheel

The other day I was driving along and happened to glance into my rear-view mirror in the professional way that I, being the expert driver I am, have trained myself to do every half hour or so. To my horror, there was a huge pickup truck less than one inch from my bumper. The driver was pulling a terrible face and it looked like he was trying to show me the little scar or something on his middle finger. Lord only knows how long he had been back there driving crazy like that. Eventually he apparently became convinced that I wasn't going to pull over and look at his finger and so he down shifted and went roaring by me mouthing words I couldn't understand.

For hours after that I could barely drive for fear that he could have been a psychopathic ax murderer or lawyer or even a psychopathic ax murdering lawyer. I worried that he looked mad enough to really severely criticize me maybe even in front of other people. Eventually I got over it and stopped shaking ultimately figuring that he was probably just an isolated nut case and that even if he was crazy, he had probably decided that I was too frail to survive a beating and so he just left me alone.

Pretty soon I forgot about the whole thing. (If you knew me, you would know that pretty soon, I forget nearly everything.) A few minutes later, I looked in the rear-view mirror again and to my surprise and consternation, although it was a different guy driving a different car, I was observing exactly the same bizarre behavior being repeated. Again, after a while, this angry driver decided not to beat me up and sped away. After the usual time to settle down, once again, I put this second experience behind me and went about my business.

Strangely, not much later, the same thing happened a third time only, if you can imagine, this time it was a young lady who was waiving her middle finger at me appearing to threaten to do terrible things and this time, I think I understood some of the words she was mouthing. I was alarmed and disgusted at her lack of culture and I concluded that I was beginning to observe an alarming, albeit consistent pattern of behavior.

As you can probably imagine, I was so perplexed, that I finally got out of my car to look and see if someone had stuck a "Honk and flip me off and act like you want to kill me if you're having a bad day" bumper sticker on my car as a practical joke. Nothing was there except the usual clumps of small animal fur and patches of rust.

I was baffled. Since that time, this has become a regularly recurring event in my life. Something like this happens nearly every time I get into my car. And the truth is, for a while I had absolutely no idea who is behind it. For all I knew it could have been part of the vast right wing conspiracy.

I know what some of you might be thinking and you can forget it because It isn't that I'm a bad driver. In my opinion, I have always been the best driver I know. I constantly drive very slowly and cautiously, way below the recommended speed limit. I usually begin signaling to turn many miles in advance, often when I first get into the car. And whenever I get lost or disoriented, I stop right where I am, even if its in the middle of the road, to await instructions from my wife, and if she's not there, to wait until help comes.

As you can see, this bad behavior by other

drivers can be a terrifying and disturbing problem. I've been left to ponder what it is that is at the root of it. After much of this pondering, it finally dawned on me what is causing it. I have concluded that it must be age discrimination. I figure that since no one is allowed to discriminate against minorities, women, foreigners, nuts, wack-os and odd or scary neighbors any more, this pent up frustration from not being allowed to exercise a person's natural inclination to make fun of people who are different and call them names has caused tremendous stress in our culture. This stress has burst out and is causing people to channel their frustration in a deviant direction, towards older senior citizen drivers.

Ha! We oldsters are smarter than you think. This is illegal age discrimination and we're not going to take it any more. If any of the rest of you senior citizens have had these experiences like me, it's time that we banded together. I propose the following:

First, we need to hire a team of mean lawyers to begin looking after our rights. I'm going to have them sue to have more people over 70 allowed to play in the NBA and the NFL. I think the president should always have somebody over 90 on his cabinet...like Jesse Helmes and if he dies before this goes to print, they should get his father.

Then, we need to sue to make sure that there are the same number of old people in all management positions with major companies in proportion to their number in society. Since 48 percent of the people in America are over 65, 48 percent of the actors and actresses on TV should be over 65. All police forces, military special units and beer commercials should be forced to have a minimum of 48 percent of their number made up of senior citizens. And, of course, every time anything bad happens to an old person, or any time an older person is passed over for a promotion, raise, or as a lottery winner, we're going to sue and say that it is discrimination that is behind it...and then I am making up some bumper stickers which say "Geezing is not a crime."

I now want all of you senior citizens everywhere to stand up...or if you can't stand up, at least motion for someone to bring you the phone so you can call the president with your experiences and complain about this discrimination. He will feel your pain and know just what to do. And whenever you spot weird behavior on the road, think up something to mouth right back at them like the words to "My Way" by Frank Sinatra. ◆

Entomologists make better Lovers!

12 How to Tweak Other Drivers

In America today, annoying other people has become one of our favorite pastimes. Getting on other people's nerves, or "tweaking" is now right up there with basketball, banjo playing, and bad haircuts as a skill in which Americans have far surpassed the rest of the world.

The following is a list of some of the premier methods of tweaking that we have experienced or thought of which happen when you're driving. As you travel down life's highways, not only do we hope that all of the cats you run over belong to people you hate, but we also hope that if you are the type of person who really likes to annoy other drivers, to be a complete butt...and hey, let's be honest, there must be thousands of you out there, you can put some of these good ideas to use. We should mention that some of these methods you'll recognize as having been used by real professionals. They have undoubtedly used them to tweak you.

How to tweak other drivers:

Tweaking Tip 1. Drive 15 MPH UNDER the speed limit in the inside lane and in the blind spot of the semi in the outside lane so no one can get past the two of you.

Tweaking Tip 2. Follow so closely that there is less than 3 inches between your front bumper and the rear bumper of the driver in front of you. (Be alert because if he should decide to slow down or stop, you may need to do so too.)

Tweaking Tip 3. Throw a very human-looking dummy out of your car.

Tweaking Tip 4. Whenever you're driving on a two lane highway, if you're in a place where it's dangerous or impossible to pass, slow way down and then when you get to where the other cars try to pass you, speed back up and race them.

Tweaking Tip 5. Let your dog drive your pickup.

Tweaking Tip 6. Pull into the emergency lane and pretend to fix a tire during rush hour. This will cause cars to slow down and look causing a major traffic jam endangering many lives.

Tweaking Tip 7. Tie a 100 foot rope to your back bumper and then connect a bed on wheels or a refrigerator onto the other end of the rope.

Tweaking Tip 8. Put out orange cones or barrels closing off all but one lane of traffic for 22 miles...and lower the speed limit to 25 all for no apparent reason.

Tweaking Tip 9. While stopped at a red light turn off your car and when the light turns green again pretend that it won't start. Then, just as the light turns yellow again, speed away leaving others to wait for the next light.

Tweaking Tip 10. Pull your son's plastic gun out from under the seat and point it at the driver you're trying to tweak.

Tweaking Tip 11. Weave in and out of the white dots in the middle of the road.

Tweaking Tip 12. Always drive the correct direction but do it in reverse. Pass as many people as you can while driving this way. ◆

13

You Probably Shouldn't Eat Stuff You Find on the Floors of Public Restrooms

As much as I travel, I feel that I must qualify as one of America's foremost experts on public rest rooms. Recently, I was driving through Colorado along Interstate 70 on a long stretch of scenic dirt and rocks. I began to notice that I was beginning to have what I would discreetly describe as a first degree lower colon alert. This feeling of slight discomfort eventually grew into a second stage alert and from there it erupted into a third stage alert or "panic". I became more worried than I would normally be during a panic because I remembered that not far up ahead was a gas station. I knew that I had but a few moments to decide whether to face the chilling horrors of a public rest room or to defy nearly 50 years of enculturation and take the action which would be safer and cleaner and just go in my pants.

Since I'm sure that many who travel have had experiences similar to this, it's time that we delve into areas which would have been considered too filthy and disgusting for us to talk about, until recently when the news which daily comes out of the white house is so disgusting that now even 5 and 6-year-olds have sufficient vocabulary to carry on an enlightened conversation with the family proctologist. Therefore, I now intend to bring this business of public rest rooms out of the old water closet, so to speak, and get it out into the open for some serious discussion.

Questions

Unfortunately a discussion is all that you get here. I am pretty much devoid of answers, I'm left with only questions such as:

1. How many different varieties of killer germs and parasites make their homes in public rest rooms? (I believe that if Congress ever does a thorough investigation of the Gulf War Syndrome, that they will re-name the problems "The Public Rest room Syndrome" instead.)

2. Why do they call them "REST" rooms? Resting is one thing that is impossible while you are crouching over the commode with wads of toilet paper stuffed up your nose to ward off the stench while trying not to let any part of the seat touch you.

3. What is the proper way to squelch those disgusting animal noises that you try so hard not to make so that the person in the stall next to you won't have an experience that he or she will want to share with everyone they know including their posterity down to their grand children? Is there a way to "throw" the noises like a ventriloquist so that they can be blamed on someone else or to make them sound like birds chirping?

4. Why are there never any clean paper towels in the dispensers?

5. Why are so many companies replacing non existent paper towels, with which you could have dried your hands, with the shell-remains of a former hair-dryer which no longer works?

6. How does one get into a public rest room, take care of business, and then get out again without touching the toilet seat or flush handle and without touching the floor with his or her feet and tracking human and sub-human decaying fecal matter bathed in urine back out to his or her car where it will have the time and proper conditions to flourish and blossom into a vicious alien creature who, upon returning home, will kill you and everyone you care about?

7. Who (or possibly what) writes and draws on bathroom walls? Moreover, what compels these perverted creatures who undoubtedly also write for the American Film Industry to empty their tiny minds on bathroom stall walls? This has troubled me for some time, and since I have thought so much about this, I do at least have some possible answers; consider:

7a. Breathing the combination of methane along with perfumed urinal pellets causes certain feeble-minded people to hallucinate and fantasize about disgusting and bizarre stuff.

7b. People with a genetic pre-disposition to pedophilia, schizophrenia and dementia along with Hollywood types, and Democratic party operatives are inspired by the ambiance in public rest rooms. For them it's like being in a mountain meadow or on the seashore and so they can't resist the urge to be creative. Or maybe reading all that other stuff inspires them.

7c. There is a society of perverted little people with telephone books who hide during the daytime behind commodes and then come out at night to do their art work, kind of like the story of the shoemaker and the elves. ◆

14

Driver's Pet Peeves

Jack "Pop" Oja from Los Angeles, California, hates having his low rider drag bottom and get high centered when he's trying to get out of the Dairy Freeze parking lot just as a rival gang is closing in.

Dexter Grovel from Frog Lick, Missouri, says he always gets upset when his brakes go out while traveling at 65 miles per hour just as the flag person steps out in front of him, often causing him to pancake that very flag person.

Steve Suerta from Cathouse, Nevada, says he gets peeved every time when, as you're driving by those orange barrels, kicking them over with your foot, you come to one that is filled with concrete.

Maggie Keyster from Mosca, Idaho, gets all bummed out every time her parents make her ride in the trunk of their '69 Volkswagen Beetle.

Jack Conejo from Frozenberg, Minnesota, despises having a semi pass you and bury you with slush, and so, because you can't see anything, you crash head-on into an over pass and die.

Stu Carne of Biffberg, Ca., doesn't like it one bit when he works during his whole 45 minute commute to get his nose clean only to sneeze all over his shirt.

Eldon Funk of Mink Breeze, Montana hates it when you hit what you thought was a large deer and then you notice the saddle and boots with spurs on.

Gordy Cabesa of El Piso, Texas

gets his underwear all in a wad whenever he's driving along in his YUGO and someone smashes into him at an angle in their Suburban and then they have the audacity to park on his head.

Andy Slothmore from Bacteria, Oregon

hates the popping sound created as you run over the thousands of toads that cover the road during mating season. The toads don't like it either.

I.B. Malo Esq., attorney from Lummox Creek, Indiana

doesn't like it whenever he stops to relieve himself at the side of the road and watches his car sail off a nearby cliff as he realizes too late that he forgot to put it in park.

Frank Bratwurst from Bladder Falls, Idaho

hates having a skunk, rat, or badger, which is chasing a cockroach, follow it into his pants leg or down his shirt while he's driving.

Renee Galletta from Boars Cheek, Texas

hates it whenever a skateboarder grabs onto her bumper just at the instant her jeep is getting leveled by a big truck.

Miss Terry Carne from Biffberg, California gets upset at having an accident that makes her swallow her cell phone...and then not being able to finish the conversation until she can get the plumber to pump out the septic tank.

Melvin Losenberger from Moose Goiter, Wyoming doesn't like getting loose clothing caught on the trailer ball and then being dragged 100 miles before someone notices.

W.J. Clinton who hails from Verminberg, Arkansas gets peeved when, after he's already put sugar into what he thought was the independent counsel's gas tank, and he notices too late that the man is now driving another car.

Viral Rampant of Boca Gigante, Florida hates smelling gas fumes and watching the passenger in her car light up.

Roy Biffwell from Dirtbath, Arizona gets all worked up when he's mooning someone in the back seat with the window down and so his mom feels a draft up front and hits the power windows.

Sue Madre from Avarice, New Jersey, hates having her mom park on top of her pet snake.

Finally, more than a few of our readers expressed how bad they hate running out of bullets in the middle of rush hour or having a rock roll off a big semi, bash in their windshield and then stay embedded in their mouth or forehead for weeks. ◆

Ask Officer Don

Officer Donald Pato , Chief of Mall Security at Fashion Atoll, is president of the American Chiropractors' Driving Academy Inc. He also is an aspiring golfer with some promise who only plays on weekends, teaches voice lessons to the deaf and is a hod carrier to stay in top shape and earn a little extra money.

Dear Officer Pato,

I find that whenever I fall asleep behind the wheel strange things happen. Sometimes I wake up hours later in a totally different time zone often in a strange room in the hospital. The other day I even woke up upside down in a public swimming pool. Is this normal? What can I do?

Sleepy in Syracuse

Dear Sleepy,

You sound pretty normal to me...assuming you mutated from a anemone spore on the planet Krypton. I know people who have solved their sleeping problem by simply removing their windshield. They found that having something to do like digging the bugs out of their eyes and teeth usually kept them awake. If that doesn't work, you can always run a tube into your car that is connected to the tail pipe. You will probably find that the smell of the exhaust is so bad it will keep you awake...for a little while.

Dear Officer Don

Whenever I drive, I have this habit of running over small animals. This makes me feel bad. What can I do?

Signed, Guilty from Gravel Falls

Dear Guilt,

I know that there are some ill-informed people who feel bad about squishing little animals. However, I believe that's only because they don't have all the facts. In the first place, scientists have proven that cats, don't mind being run over. They have no brain. Also, there are many animals such as, snow leopard , Bengal tiger, ermine, spotted owl, snail darter and lynx, to name just a few, which have coats worth millions on the black market. If you ever run over one of those dudes, take the time to stop and skin that sucker. You'll be glad you did.

Dear Officer Pato,

When I was a boy years ago riding my scooter in a 100 year snowstorm, this big semi truck went flying by at 70 MPH and splatted slop all over me. I couldn't see, so I ran off the road into a snow bank. From this experience I eventually began to have terrible emotional problems and completely lost my mind and became accountant for the DNC. Now, I have this eternal hatred for all truck drivers and Vespa motor scooters. I would like to be able to put this behind me and get on with life but I don't know how.

Signed, Neurotic from Newark

Dear NeuRot,

What you are suffering from has been clinically diagnosed as being a wimpy brainless snot-nosed twirp. It sounds to me like it's probably terminal. You sound like someone who should just bag life, get an ugly haircut, sag your pants and spend the rest of your life hanging out on a skateboard.

Dear Officer Donald,

I drive a 1984 olive green Plymouth Duster. The car dealer who sold it to me said it would be a "chick magnet". It has now been 2 months since I bought it and I still can't seem to get any girls. Do I have grounds to sue? (I've been told I'm also a terrific ballroom dancer and I play a mean accordion.)

Pathetic from Pittsburgh

Dear Tic,

Yes, you should definitely sue...first, sue the doctors who delivered you and who certainly must have dropped you on your head, second, your mom for not following her primal instincts and eating her young, and finally your father if he can be found, for taking all those drugs and that radiation treatment just before you were conceived.

Dear Don,

Just the other day I pulled up alongside a semi at a stop sign just as it was making a right turn. Now, my Ford Fiesta is pretty much nothing more than an ornament on the side of this Oscar Meyer truck. Unfortunately, the doors on the car were small to begin with and with them being smashed and all, I can't seem to get out. I am calling you on my cell phone. Could you please tell me what to do?

P.S. I'm starting to get bored being witness to hundreds of wiener deliveries.

Signed, Smashed in Salt Lake

Dear Smashed,

Don't worry, sometime in the next few hours or days the truck you are stuck on will need to make another right turn. If there is a stop sign or anything alongside the road when he does, it will scrape you off the side of the truck like a windshield wiper scrapes off a bug.

Dear Officer Pato,

My right turn signal has been stuck signaling a left turn since November of 1966. How can I fix this problem?

Signed, Dipstick from Delta

Dear Dip,

Next time you stop, just get out of your car and pick up a hammer or a big rock and smash in that light. Odds are that no one will care any way because in case you haven't noticed, no one ever uses their turn signals any more. ◆

'The Truth About Life' Humor Books

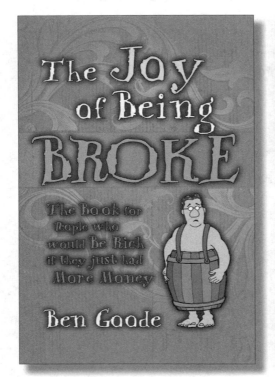

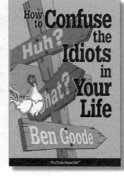

Order Online! www.apricotpress.com

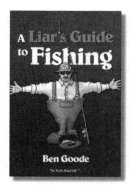

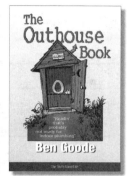

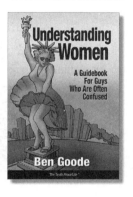

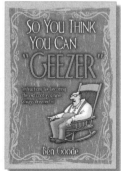

Apricot Press Order Form

Book Title	Quantity	x	Cost / Book	=	Total
_____	_____		_____		_____
_____	_____		_____		_____
_____	_____		_____		_____
_____	_____		_____		_____
_____	_____		_____		_____
_____	_____		_____		_____
_____	_____		_____		_____
_____	_____		_____		_____

All Humor Books are $6.95 US.   **All Cook Books are $9.95 US.**

Do not send Cash. Mail check or money order to:
**Apricot Press   P.O. Box 98
Nephi, Utah   84648**
Telephone 435-623-1929
Allow 3 weeks for delivery.

**Quantity discounts available.
Call us for more information.**
9 a.m. - 5 p.m. MST

Sub Total =

Shipping =   **$2.00**

Tax 8.5% =

Total Amount
Enclosed =

Shipping Address

Name:

Street:

City: State:

Zip Code:

Telephone:

Email: